THE FORCE OF VISION

"Where there is no vision, the people perish:
but he that keepeth the law,
happy is he."

Proverb 29:18

By
Franklin N Abazie

The Force Of Vision

COPYRIGHT 2017 by Franklin N Abazie
ISBN: 978:1-945-133-42-8

All right reserved. This book or any portion thereof may not be reproduced or used in any manner whatsoever without the express written permission of the publisher, except for the use of brief quotations in a book review. All Bible quotes are from King James Version and others as noted.

Published by: F N ABAZIE PUBLISHING HOUSE- a.k.a Empowerment Bookstore.

That I may publish with the voice of thanksgiving and tell of all thy wondrous works.
Psalms 26:7

To order additional copies, wholesales or booking: Call the Church office 973-372-7518, or call Empowerment Bookstore Hotline 973-393-8518

Worship address: 343 Sanford Avenue Newark New Jersey 07106
Administrative Head Office address: 33 Schley Street Newark New Jersey 07112
Email:pastorfranknto@yahoo.com
Website www.fnabaziehealingministries.org

Publishing House: www.fnabaziepublishinghouse.org

This book is a production of F N Abazie Publishing House.
A publication Arms of Miracle of God Ministries 2017
First Edition

CONTENTS

THE MANDATE OF THE COMMISSION............iv

ARMS OF THE COMMISSION...............................v

INTRODUCTION...vi

CHAPTER 1

1. What is Vision? 26

CHAPTER 2

2. How do I fulfil God's Vision for my life...............42

CHAPTER 3

3. Prayer of Salvation..75

CHAPTER 4

4. About the Author...89

THE MANDATE OF THE COMMISSION

"The moment is due to impact your world through the revival of the healing & miracle ministry of Jesus Christ of Nazareth. "I am sending you to restore health unto thee and I will heal thee of thy wounds, said the Lord of Host."

ARMS OF THE COMMISSION

1) F N Abazie Ministries-Miracle of God Ministries (Miracle Chapel Intl)

2) F N Abazie TV Ministries: Global Television Ministry Outreach.

3) F N Abazie Radio Ministries: Radio Broadcasting Outreach.

4) F N Abazie Publishing House: Book Publication.

5) F N Abazie Bible School: also called Word of Healing Bible School (W.O.H.B.S)

6) F N Abazie Evangelistic Ass: Miracle of God Ministries: Global Crusade

7) Empowerment Bookstore: Book distribution.

8) F N Abazie Helping Hands: Meeting the help of the needy world wide

9) F N Abazie Disaster Recovery Mission: Global Disaster Recovery.

10) F N Abazie Prison Ministry: Prison Ministry for all convicts "Second chance"

Some of our ministry arms are waiting the appointed time to commence.

INTRODUCTION

Although I may never get the chance to meet you in person. However, through this book, I am glad to meet you. It has always been my desire to write this book ever since I discovered God's plan and purpose for my life. I was instructed by the Holy Spirit to pen down this book: The force of Vision. In this small book, you will learn of divine vision from the Lord Jesus.

Apostle Paul said *"And the men which journeyed with him stood speechless, hearing a voice, but seeing no man."* **Acts9:7.**

It is written *"And they that were with me saw indeed the light, and were afraid; but they heard not the voice of him that spake to me."* **Acts22:9**

In my own opinion, every vision from the Lord is for an appointed time. It is written *"For the vision is yet for an appointed time, but at the end it shall speak, and not lie: though it tarry, wait for it; because it will surely come, it will not tarry."* **Habakkuk2:3**

Every time God gives us a vision, we must run with it in life. For unless we run with heavenly vision. God will give it to somebody else.

It is written *"Whereupon as I went to Damascus with authority and commission from the chief priests. At midday, O king, I saw in the way a light from heaven, above the brightness of the sun, shining round about me and them which journeyed with me.*

And when we were all fallen to the earth, I heard a voice speaking unto me, and saying in the Hebrew tongue, Saul, Saul, why persecutest thou me? it is hard for thee to kick against the pricks. And I said, Who art thou, Lord? And he said, I am Jesus whom thou persecutest.

But rise, and stand upon thy feet: for I have appeared unto thee for this purpose, to make thee a minister and a witness both of these things which thou hast seen, and of those things in the which I will appear unto thee; Delivering thee from the people, and from the Gentiles, unto whom now I send thee.

To open their eyes, and to turn them from darkness to light, and from the power of Satan unto God, that they may receive forgiveness of sins, and inheritance among them which are sanctified by faith that is in me. Whereupon, O king Agrippa, I was not disobedient unto the heavenly vision."
Acts26:12-19

It is written *"My people are destroyed for lack of knowledge: because thou hast rejected knowledge, I will also reject thee, that thou shalt be no priest to me: seeing thou hast forgotten the law of thy God, I will also forget thy children."*
Hosea4:6.

I believe everyone should at least know what they are called to do in life. Most folks go about doing what is comfortable for them but not what is commanded by the Lord. It is written *"So I prophesied as he commanded me, and the breath came into them, and they lived, and stood up upon their feet, an exceeding great army."*
Ezekiel37:10

"Therefore my people are gone into captivity, because they have no knowledge: and their honourable men are famished, and their multitude dried up with thirst."
Isaiah 5:13

Often most of us misinterpret heavenly vision for the discernment of Spirit. Or the word of wisdom. I like you to neglect my grammar but pay close attention to the context of this text. Come with me as the Holy Spirit reveals to us the force of a vision from God. It is my prayer, that we all capture God's plan and purpose for our life in the Mighty Name of Jesus.

Happy Reading.

HIS DESTINY WAS THE CROSS….

HIS PURPOSE WAS LOVE…..

HIS REASON WAS YOU….

WE MUST EMULATE THE LIFE OF THE EAGLE

~Eagles fly alone and at a high altitude

We must always stay away from narrow-minded people, those that bring us down. We must always keep good company if we must fulfil God's vision for our life. For unless we think great, we will never become great in life. We must always set a standard for ourselves.

~Eagles have an accurate vision.

We must always remain focused regardless of the prevailing obstacle opposing us in life. As long as your vision is not from the Lord, it will not be accurate.

~Eagles do not eat dead meat. They feed on only fresh prey.

We must never rely on our past accomplishment. We must always seek for new frontiers to conquer in life.

As long as you look ahead and think ahead in life, you will eventually move ahead in life.

~Eagles are comfortable in the storm

Those who achieve great things in life are never afraid of challenges in life. One man said "what you fail to confront you cannot conquer" .Most great men see opportunities in every challenge or obstacle in life.

~Female eagles seek for commitment in relationship with the male.

Whether it's our personal life or professional life, we must always look for commitment with people we intend to partner or establish a relationship together.

~Eagles prepare for training

I heard a preacher said one time "for unless we learn we cannot earn more." Often we desire a change in life but not ready to train for it. In this kingdom life is practical and not mystical.

For unless you are trained you will not be able to fulfil your God given vision in life. We must be determine to train ourselves in order to fulfil our God given vision in life.

~The eagles sheds his/her feathers as she ages in life for new ones.

We must always shed off-all old bad habits. Some of our old habit got to go as we mature and age in life. We must be open and willing to embrace change in life with joy and gratitude.

We must be willing to take healthy risks in life. If we win, we can lead; if we lose, we can guide other with our experience.

People are not what they say, but what they do; so judge them not from their words but from their actions.

When someone hurts you, don't feel bad because it's a law of nature that the tree that bears the sweetest fruits gets maximum number of stones.

Take whatever you can from your life because when life starts taking from you, it takes even your last breath.

~Eagles are comfortable in the storm

Those who achieve great things in life are never afraid of challenges in life. One man said "what you fail to confront you cannot conquer" .Most great men see opportunities in every challenge or obstacle in life.

~Female eagles seek for commitment in relationship with the male.

Whether it's our personal life or professional life, we must always look for commitment with people we intend to partner or establish a relationship together.

~Eagles prepare for training

I heard a preacher said one time "for unless we learn we cannot earn more." Often we desire a change in life but not ready to train for it. In this kingdom life is practical and not mystical.

For unless you are trained you will not be able to fulfil your God given vision in life. We must be determine to train ourselves in order to fulfil our God given vision in life.

~The eagles sheds his/her feathers as she ages in life for new ones.

We must always shed off-all old bad habits. Some of our old habit got to go as we mature and age in life. We must be open and willing to embrace change in life with joy and gratitude.

We must be willing to take healthy risks in life. If we win, we can lead; if we lose, we can guide other with our experience.

People are not what they say, but what they do; so judge them not from their words but from their actions.

When someone hurts you, don't feel bad because it's a law of nature that the tree that bears the sweetest fruits gets maximum number of stones.

Take whatever you can from your life because when life starts taking from you, it takes even your last breath.

In this world, people will always throw stones on the path of your success. It depends on what you make from them - a wall or a bridge.

Challenges make life interesting; overcoming them make life meaningful.

There is no joy in victory without running the risk of defeat.

A path without obstacles leads nowhere.

Past is a nice place to visit but certainly not a good place to stay.

You can't have a better tomorrow if you are thinking about yesterday all the time.

If what you did yesterday still looks big to you, then you haven't done much today.

If you don't build your dreams, someone else will hire you to build theirs.

If you don't climb the mountain; you can't view the plain.

Don't leave it idle - use your brain.

You are not paid for having brain, you are only rewarded for using it intelligently.

It is not what you don't have that limits you; it is what you have but don't know how to use.

What you fail to learn might teach you a lesson.

The difference between a corrupt person and an honest person is: The corrupt person has a price while the honest person has a value.

If you succeed in cheating someone, don't think that the person is a fool...... Realize that the person trusted you much more than you deserved.

Honesty is an expensive gift; don't expect it from cheap people

HOW TO MAKE AN IMPACT IN LIFE

We must first believe in God for faith in Him, to work for our lives. We must be action oriented because faith is action oriented in my opinion. Nothing changes in life until we take action in life.

If we claim to have faith, then we must be action ready to move into the supernatural. We must always trust and have confidence in God and in ourselves. Nobody is our God, therefore never trust on anybody in life.

We must always believe in God and in our own abilities to get things accomplish in life. We must first discover ourselves before others discover the talents in us. We must recognize our strength and weakness before we make certain decisions in life.

You are certain to get the worst of the bargain when you exchange ideas with the wrong person.

In this race of life, always make friends with those who can inspire you, those you can learn from. The bible says He that walketh with wise men shall be wise: but a companion of fools shall be destroyed

Try to always be able to differentiate those God planted into your life for a season and for a long term. Information and continual learning is the key to succeed in life. Always chose your friends wisely, for evil companion corrupt good manners.

Remember "he that walk with the wise shall be wise."

In the time of prosperity we recognize our friends. *"Wealth maketh many friends"*. **Proverb19:4**

But in the time of adversity our friends know us. *"and there is a friend that sticketh closer than a brother"*.**Proverb18:24**

Always recognize those who make you a special person in their lives. Never make people significant in your life when you are only an option to them. The less you associate with some people the more your life will improve. Remember Abraham did not become rich until he separated from lot his nephew.

"And the Lord said unto Abram, after that Lot was separated from him, Lift up now thine eyes, and look from the place where thou art northward, and southward, and eastward, and westward: For all the land which thou seest, to thee will I give it, and to thy seed forever."

Genesis 13:14-15

Anytime time you allow mediocrity in others, it increases your mediocrity. An important attribute in successful people is their impatience with failure, negative thinking, and mediocrity. As we grow in life, our association will eventually change over time.

Eventually, you will disconnect from those that failed to improve their lives and you will connect and make friends with other successful people going up higher in the race of life. Never receive counsel from unproductive negative thinking people, never discus your trial and challenges with those incapable of contributing to the solution or solving your problems.

Always look for the best in people around you. Develop a forgiving heart, a thankful countenance, and praiseful spirit.

Always remember this, if you are going to achieve excellence in big things, you must develop the habit in little matters.

Collin Powell once said and I quote "A dream doesn't become a reality through magic, it takes sweat, determination, and hard work." There is no secret to success, it is the result of preparation, hard work, and learning from failure."

Excellence is not an exception, it is a prevailing attitude.

We must develop the habit of confronting all prevailing challenges facing our lives. Remember there is always away OUT for you, there is also away UP for you and away FORWARD for us all in life as long as we believe in God and have faith.

HOW DO I RECEIVE HEAVENLY VISION?

It is written *"If any of you lack wisdom, let him ask of God, that giveth to all men liberally, and upbraideth not; and it shall be given him."* **James1:5**

Every genuine vision from God, must come from the Lord. Although, most visionaries men and women who impacted the way we live today, most never receive any vision from the Lord. These great men/women impacted our lives with their vision because of the power of a heart desire.

If you truly want something done excellently, you will go out of your way to make it happen.

On the contrary every vision for the preaching and teaching of the gospel of Jesus Christ must come from the Lord.

~The power of a heart desire

Besides hearing from the Lord, there is always a heart desire. What is God saying to us asper our heart desire. Is there any peculiar desire from the Lord in your heart? For unless you pursue that desire and fulfil it, you will never have a rest of mind. It is written The desire accomplished is sweet to the soul:…**Proverb13:19**

~The power of a mental picture

In my own opinion, mental pictures are the short cut into breakthrough. Abram was promised, that as far as his eyes can see, God will give it to him.

Every time we form a mental picture in our heart, we cannot go wrong in life.

Although there are negative and positive mental pictures in life, but every time we develop a mental picture in life as believers, it is also for the promotion of the Kingdom of God.

~ The power of a mentor

It is written *"And he said unto them, Look on me, and do likewise: and, behold, when I come to the outside of the camp, it shall be that, as I do, so shall ye do."*

Judges 7:17.

The power of a mentor is the short cut into divine vision. It is written *"And there shall be, like people, like priest: and I will punish them for their ways, and reward them their doings."*

Hosea 4:9

~The Power of a dream

Every time God gives us a vision through the power of a dream, we cannot go wrong in life.

It is written *" For God speaketh once, yea twice, yet man perceiveth it not. In a dream, in a vision of the night, when deep sleep falleth upon men, in slumberings upon the bed; Then he openeth the ears of men, and sealeth their instruction."*

Job 33:14-16

CHAPTER 1

What is a Vision?

"For the vision is yet for an appointed time, but at the end it shall speak, and not lie: though it tarry, wait for it; because it will surely come, it will not tarry."

Habakkuk 2:3

Every time we mention the word Vision, most of us thinks of the state of being able to see things in the physical realm. In the context of this book "vision" means our ability to see ahead through the power of God-in a dream, through an audible voice, a revelation, or in a trance.

God's vision can be communicated to us either through a dream or trance, or as a supernatural apparition. For any vision to make an impact, the visionary must be goal oriented and success driven.

The term vision has numerous applications, depending upon one's perspective.

Chapter 1 - What is a Vison?

From a biblical angle it may be used to describe an actual vision or revelation from God.

To the unbeliever the term is often used in a skeptical or derogatory way. For example, they would argue that the resurrection appearances of Christ were merely "visions," i.e., internal phenomena having no objective reality or even necessarily any reality at all, something like hallucinations

Although most of us genuinely have a vision from the Lord, but until we are devoted, disciplined, dedicated the vision will tarry. It is written *" Verily, verily, I say unto you, Except a corn of wheat fall into the ground and die, it abideth alone: but if it die, it bringeth forth much fruit."* **John12:24.**

For unless we are ready to pay the price for any vision, we will never make an impact with such vision. Unless you are driven by the vision you receive from the Lord, you will be employed to fulfil someone's vision in life.

It is written *"For I would that all men were even as I myself. But every man hath his proper gift of God, one after this manner, and another after that."*

1cor7:7.

Our stardom will only shine whenever we genuinely discover and pursue Divine Vision. Most of us crash in life, because we pursue the vision of our friends and mentors in life.

But until we face our own future with love, compassion, and gratitude, we will never make an impact in our life time. Every one of us is called by the Lord. It is written *"For many are called, but few are chosen."*

Mathew22:14.

The Holy Scripture gave us strict guidelines to follow in other to fulfil our heavenly calling.

Chapter 1 - What is a Vison?

It is written *"Wherefore the rather, brethren, give diligence to make your calling and election sure: for if ye do these things, ye shall never fall:"* **2Peter1:10**

Every one of us have a heavenly vision. But unless we discover it for our lives, we will struggle and be opposed with challenges in life.

"Who hath saved us, and called us with an holy calling, not according to our works, but according to his own purpose and grace, which was given us in Christ Jesus before the world began."

2tim1:9

Without doubt God had distributed spiritual gift to everyone.

Jeremiah said *"Before I formed thee in the belly I knew thee; and before thou camest forth out of the womb I sanctified thee, and I ordained thee a prophet unto the nations."*

Jeremiah1:5

Apostle Paul said *"But when it pleased God, who separated me from my mother's womb, and called me by his grace."*

Gal1:15

There is no doubt in my heart. I know you are called by God. There is a heavenly assignment concerning your life here on earth. But have you discovered it? Or you are still wondering what to do about your future?

"For I would that all men were even as I myself. But every man hath his proper gift of God, one after this manner, and another after that."

1cor7:7

"But as God hath distributed to every man, as the Lord hath called every one, so let him walk. And so ordain I in all churches."

1cor7:17

Chapter 1 - What is a Vison?

"Let every man abide in the same calling wherein he was called."

1cor7:20

"Brethren, let every man, wherein he is called, therein abide with God."

1cor7:24

It is written *"And he said, Hear now my words: If there be a prophet among you, I the Lord will make myself known unto him in a vision, and will speak unto him in a dream."*

Number12:6

As believers every one of us must develop a vivid mental image of our future. *"If you can see ahead, know ahead, you will go ahead in life."* Often most of us go to school to pursue a career chosen by our father, or older brother.

For unless we make an early choice in life we will end up in confusion. Vision therefore helps us to make a choice and stick to our choice in life.

Although Vision is essential for organizations and companies. It is recommended that we develop our personal vision in life. However, God's vision must be dynamic and not static.

No one just wakes up early in the morning and says, God gave me a vision to become a preacher this morning. For any vision to speak, there must be a clear calling from God. Secondly there must be a burning desire to fulfil such vision from the Lord.

We must train ourselves diligently in order to fulfil such a vision from the Lord.

The Significance of a Vision from God

~Vision enhances focus and promotes unity.

Often some of us wander in confusion life. I know of a family member who literally did almost every profession you can think about in life. If I am permitted to say it this way.

Chapter 1 - What is a Vison?

"Where there is no vision, the people end up in confusion in life." Every time you have a genuine vision from God it helps us to be focused in life.

Jesus said *"For where two or three are gathered together in my name, there am I in the midst of them."*

Mathew18:20.

I recommend that we develop a genuine vision from the Lord. May you never end up Jack of all trades, master of none.

~God's Vision makes us responsible in life

Men of vision are responsible men of impact in life. Visionaries are men and women who transform the world. Innovators like Mike Zuckerberg, Bill gates will forever be remembered for generation to come.

~God's Vision Provides Purpose

Often some of us have no purpose in life. Every time you genuinely have a vision from God, it gives you purpose for living.

~God's vision brings out the leadership quality inside of us

As a visionary your leadership skill will be tested. Most church founders start a church and seven to ten years later, the church closes. Not because they could not pray correctly. But because they lacked the leadership structure and skill to move the ministry into the next level.

Hindrances to a divine vision from the Lord

------------------------Doubt----------------------

Some church folks make me laugh. How can you receive a vision from the Lord Jesus, and at the same time you are doubting if you should run with your vision.

Others go to school and get academic degrees yet feel unqualified to function in any capacity. Every time we doubt, it is not from the Lord.

Chapter 1 - What is a Vison?

For as long as we doubt our calling it will not be fulfilled in our life time.

It is written *"A double minded man is unstable in all his ways."*

James1:8

--------------------- **Unbelief**---------------------

As long as you do not believe, you will struggle to identify with your calling in life. Every time we don't believe in ourselves. We paralyze our heavenly call**ing.**

Talking about Jesus the bible says *"And he could there do no mighty work, save that he laid his hands upon a few sick folk, and healed them. And he marvelled because of their unbelief. And he went round about the villages, teaching."*

Mark6:5-6.

Fear

There are always opposition in life to any vision from God. The truth is most people are afraid of nothing. Fear of the unknown will make most people not to pursue their heavenly calling in life.

"Thou therefore gird up thy loins, and arise, and speak unto them all that I command thee: be not dismayed at their faces, lest I confound thee before them."

Jer1:17

Apostle Paul said *"For a great door and effectual is opened unto me, and there are many adversaries."*

1cor16:9

Sin

As simple as it can be sin is sin. It will hinder anyone from fulfilling our heavenly calling in life. Sin should never dominate our lives as believers.

(See Romans6:14)

Chapter 1 - What is a Vison?

It is written *"Ye adulterers and adulteresses, know ye not that the friendship of the world is enmity with God? whosoever therefore will be a friend of the world is the enemy of God."*
James4:4

WE MUST REPENT OF OUR SINS

"Wherefore seeing we also are compassed about with so great a cloud of witnesses, let us lay aside every weight, and the sin which doth so easily beset us, and let us run with patience the race that is set before us"

Hebrew12:1.

We must not allow sin to destroy our calling and destiny in life. We must therefore repent of any known sin in our lives before God can restore our destiny.

"For sin shall not have dominion over you: for ye are not under the law, but under grace."
Romans6:14

"Every time we yield to sin, we place ourselves in captivity. We must all strive to forsake sin and do away with every evil that dent our Christian dignity. Know ye not, that to whom ye yield yourselves servants to obey, his servants ye are to whom ye obey; whether of sin unto death, or of obedience unto righteousness?"

Romans 6:16

It is written *"Be not overcome of evil, but overcome evil with good."*

Romans 12:21.

We must all repent of any know sin that dents our Christian walk with the Lord Jesus Christ.

Apostle Paul had this to say….

"I find then a law, that, when I would do good, evil is present with me. For I delight in the law of God after the inward man: But I see another law in my members, warring against the law of my mind, and bringing me into captivity to the law of sin which is in my

Chapter 1 - What is a Vison?

members. O wretched man that I am! who shall deliver me from the body of this death? I thank God through Jesus Christ our Lord. So then with the mind I myself serve the law of God; but with the flesh the law of sin."

Romans 7:21-25

The above scripture makes a lot of sin if you examine your own life. Evil is present every time we strive to do good. What shall we say then? Shall we continue in sin, that grace may abound? God forbid. How shall we, that are dead to sin, live any longer therein? **Romans 6:1-2**

"Examine yourselves, whether ye be in the faith; prove your own selves. Know ye not your own selves, how that Jesus Christ is in you, except ye be reprobates?"

2cor 13:5

Although most faith people live in denial about the work of the flesh, from my own scriptural understanding everyone operating within the scope of Galatians 5:20-21 is classified as a sinner.

How to I come out of sin?

Although we are all sinners, it takes a will power of the mind for us to repent and come out of sin. So many people and died because they could not let go the sin that easily best them go. Preacher who used to drug addicts have crashed and died because they went back into their addiction.

A great man of God who repented because of alcohol in the family died of excessive alcohol abuse. We must make up our mind for good if we must come out of sin. We must confess, and forsake it in the mighty name of Jesus.

You must **REPENT** and **CONFESS & PROCLAIM THE LORD JESUS CHRIST**

The word says as many as received him, to them gave He power to become the sons of God. Even to them that believe on his name.

Chapter 1 - What is a Vison?

To qualify for divine visitation do the following sincerely,

1) Acknowledge that you are a sinner and that He died for you. **Rom3:23.**

2) Repent of your sins. **Acts 3:19, Luke13:5, 2Peter3:9**

3) Believe in your heart that Jesus died for your sin. **Romans10:10**

4) Confess Jesus as the Lord over your life. **Romans10:10, Acts2:21**

Now repeat this Prayer after me

Say Lord Jesus, I accept you today, as my Lord and my savior, forgive me of my sins wash me with your blood. Right now, I believe, I am sanctified, I am save, I am free, I am free from the Power of sin to serve the Lord Jesus. Thank you Lord for saving me. Amen.

Congratulation: **YOU ARE NOW A BORN AGAIN CHRISTIAN**

CHAPTER 2

How do I fulfil God's Vision for my life?

"Where there is no vision, the people perish: but he that keepeth the law, happy is he." **Prover29:18**

In order for us to answer the above question, we must first genuinely ask ourselves, what do I enjoy doing? What do I love to do from my heart? Often what we love to do in life is not the will of God for our life. To fulfil God's vision for our lives, we must be sincere, obedient, loyal, and submissive to the will of God over our lives.

We must carefully search our heart and know if what we call vision is ambition, self-desire, or a real vision from God. Every time God calls anyone God makes the provision available to fulfil the work. To fulfil divine vision therefore we must note the following: Know genuinely that the vision is from the Lord.

Chapter 2 - How do I Fulfil God's Vision for my Life?

More also, we must be proactive about the vision.

For anyone of us to fulfil our heaven calling, we must develop a burning desire and compassion for whatever is that assignment. We must go out of our way to do research on those topics to see what others who had the same calling did in their life time.

Finally we must develop a mentor and mentee relationship. Either by reading book of known authors or by seating under anyone we consider to be a master in that area of our calling in Christ Jesus.

The truth is, those who discovered their God given vision early in life rise to stardom before their fortieth birthday. You will struggle for ever unless you comply with divine plan concerning your life. One of the cheapest ways to pursue divine vision for our life is to read books.

One man said that information plus revelation will give you revolution. As long as you are ignorant of the truth, you will struggle to identify with divine plan for your life.

It is written *"Lest Satan should get an advantage of us: for we are not ignorant of his devices."*

2cor2:11

If you miss your heavenly vision, you will forever struggle in life. God's plan and purpose is the reason you were born.

It is written *"Before I formed thee in the belly I knew thee; and before thou camest forth out of the womb I sanctified thee, and I ordained thee a prophet unto the nations."*

Jer1:5

Every one of us is called by God to fulfil one assignment or the other.

Chapter 2 - How do I Fulfil God's Vision for my Life?

It is written *"For many are called, but few are chosen."*

Mathew22:14

It is our responsibility therefore to diligently identity, and pursue the call or vision of God upon our life on time.

"Who hath saved us, and called us with an holy calling, not according to our works, but according to his own purpose and grace, which was given us in Christ Jesus before the world began"

2tim1:9

Dr. Myles Monroe once said,

"I think that the greatest gift God ever gave man is not the gift of sight but the gift of vision," Dr. Myles Munroe says. *"Sight is a function of the eyes, but vision is a function of the heart. When a person doesn't have a vision, they live by their eyes. That means we live by what we see.*

That's one of the reasons why people are so depressed, and that's why the future never becomes a reality. "Vision is a source of hope; it's the source of courage; it's the source of perseverance in the midst of difficulty."---**Dr. Myles Monroe**

How do I acknowledge God's vision for your life?

~We must surrender our life to the will God

Unless we surrender our life to the will of God, we will forever live in frustration. The struggle will not end until you discover God's plan for your life.

One man said you will be battered in life if you do not follow God's pattern. You will never be at ease until you are in the center of God's plan for your life.

It is written *"For I know the thoughts that I think toward you, saith the Lord, thoughts of peace, and not of evil, to give you an expected end."* **Jer 29:11**

Chapter 2 - How do I Fulfil God's Vision for my Life?

~We must confess any known sin in our life

Scriptures told us that if we confess our sin, He is faithful and just to forgive us our sins. As long as there is sin in your life, you will struggle with almost everything in your life. David said *"If I regard iniquity in my heart, the Lord will not hear me."*

The scripture cannot be broken. The bitter truth is that you will not prosper as long as there is sin in your life.

It is written *"He that covereth his sins shall not prosper: but whoso confesseth and forsaketh them shall have mercy."* **Proverb 28:13**

~We must seek the face of God through prayer, fasting, and worship.

God's plan and purpose for our life will remain ineffective and impotent as long as we ignore prayer and fasting.

For unless we seek the face of God through prayer, and fasting, we will not witnessed fulfillment of the appointed heaven mandate for our lives.

~We must search the Scriptures for the revealed will of God.

God plan and purpose concerning our lives is written in the Holy bible. Until you discover it, you will remain in frustration.

~We must submit to the help of the Holy Spirit.

Most of us do not want to submit to anyone. But unless you submit to the Holy Ghost you will not be able to fulfil God's vision concerning our life.

~We must carefully and reasonably evaluate our gift from God, heart desire and area of strength in life

For unless we seek the face of God through prayer, and fasting, we will not witnessed fulfillment of the appointed heaven mandate for our lives.

~We must search the Scriptures for the revealed will of God.

God plan and purpose concerning our lives is written in the Holy bible. Until you discover it, you will remain in frustration.

~We must submit to the help of the Holy Spirit.

Most of us do not want to submit to anyone. But unless you submit to the Holy Ghost you will not be able to fulfil God's vision concerning our life.

~We must carefully and reasonably evaluate our gift from God, heart desire and area of strength in life

One man said you will be battered in life if you do not follow God's pattern. You will never be at ease until you are in the center of God's plan for your life.

It is written *"For I know the thoughts that I think toward you, saith the Lord, thoughts of peace, and not of evil, to give you an expected end."*

Jer29:11

~We must confess any known sin in our life

Scriptures told us that if we confess our sin, He is faithful and just to forgive us our sins. As long as there is sin in your life, you will struggle with almost everything in your life.

David said *"If I regard iniquity in my heart, the Lord will not hear me."*

The scripture cannot be broken. The bitter truth is that you will not prosper as long as there is sin in your life.

It is written *"He that covereth his sins shall not prosper: but whoso confesseth and forsaketh them shall have mercy."*

Proverb28:13

Chapter 2 - How do I Fulfil God's Vision for my Life?

Most of us waste our time in the wrong job, career, and marriage. Often most talented people are blinded from the truth. We tend to pursue desires and careers in the area where God did not call us. Again for unless we are in the center of God's plan, we will never be fulfilled in life.

~We must be practical with any vision we received from the Lord.

It is foolishness to be mystical about any vision we receive from the Lord. Remember… God is the all wise God. As believers we must be smart, responsible, and practical in our approach to any vision we receive from the Lord.

HINDRANCE TO THE WILL OF GOD

Disobedient

"Whereupon, O king Agrippa, I was not disobedient unto the heavenly vision." **Acts26:19**

As long as you live in dissidence you have no chance to fulfil Gods plan and purpose for your life. If you do not want to end up struggling in life, you must obey the will of God for your life.

Un-willing to learn

As long as you are not willing to learn, you will end up a fool. God's plan and purpose will be withhold from anyone who is not humble and willing to learn from their superior.

ACCESS INTO THE SUPERNATURAL

BE BORN AGAIN

We must be born again for us to experience the supernatural and mentorship.

"Jesus answered and said unto him, Verily, verily, I say unto thee, Except a man be born again, he cannot see the kingdom of God. Nicodemus saith unto him, How can a man be born when he is old? can he enter the second time into his mother's womb, and be born?

Chapter 2 - How do I Fulfil God's Vision for my Life?

Jesus answered, Verily, verily, I say unto thee, Except a man be born of water and of the Spirit, he cannot enter into the kingdom of God.

That which is born of the flesh is flesh; and that which is born of the Spirit is spirit. Marvel not that I said unto thee, Ye must be born again. The wind bloweth where it listeth, and thou hearest the sound thereof, but canst not tell whence it cometh, and whither it goeth: so is every one that is born of the Spirit."

John3:3-8

We must therefore obey the voice of the Lord , confes him as Lord and savior then we can learn from his teaching and position our lives to encounter the supernatural.

THE FEAR OF GOD

"One of the greatest channels to position our lives to encounter the supernatural is to covet the spirit of the fear of God.

The fear of the Lord is the beginning of wisdom: and the knowledge of the holy is understanding."

Proverb9:10

RIGHTEOUS LIFESTYLE

It may take a longer time, but over the cause of your life time it will show. Righteousness is a virtue that tell everybody around you, the way you live, the way you do business and the way you operate.

"For the vision is yet for an appointed time, but at the end it shall speak, and not lie: though it tarry, wait for it; because it will surely come, it will not tarry."

Habakkuk2:3

INTEGRITY

"The integrity of the upright shall guide them……."

Proverb11:3

Chapter 2 - How do I Fulfil God's Vision for my Life?

As long as you carry integrity in your heart, it will guide your life from all assaults and attacks of the devil. So he fed them according to the integrity of his heart; and guided them by the skillfulness of his hands. **Palm78:72**

AGREEMENT

Until you agree with the Holy Spirit by believe God's word to be true, you will forever suffer frustration. Once you agree with the Holy Spirit, you are guaranteed access into the supernatural.

"Again I say unto you, That if two of you shall agree on earth as touching any thing that they shall ask, it shall be done for them of my Father which is in heaven."
Mathew18:19

"For where two or three are gathered together in my name, there am I in the midst of them."
Mathew 18:20.

"Remember .... The Lord thy God in the midst of thee is mighty."

Zeph3:17

SOUL WINNING

It is written *"…… and he that winneth souls is wise."*

Proverb11:30.

Soul winning is the gate way into the supernatural. As long as you win souls for Jesus he will decorate your life and destiny.

CONCLUSION

"Where there is no vision, the people perish: but he that keepeth the law, happy is he."

Proverb29:18

Apostle Paul said *"Whereupon, O king Agrippa, I was not disobedient unto the heavenly vision."*

Acts26:19.

Chapter 2 - How do I Fulfil God's Vision for my Life?

Before you put this book down you must ask God to reveal His plan for your life. The purpose of this book is to help you identify with your heavenly calling in life. In my own opinion, there is no doubt about your calling , but only few will be chosen.

"For many are called, but few are chosen."
Mathew22:14

"Wherefore the rather, brethren, give diligence to make your calling and election sure: for if ye do these things, ye shall never fall:"
2Peter1:9.

Who hath saved us, and called us with an holy calling, not according to our works, but according to his own purpose and grace, which was given us in Christ Jesus before the world began. **2timothy1:10**

Without purpose your life has no meaning. Every career is not for you, but there is an assignment for your life.

"For I would that all men were even as I myself. But every man hath his proper gift of God, one after this manner, and another after that."
1cor7:7

"But as God hath distributed to every man, as the Lord hath called every one, so let him walk. And so ordain I in all churches."
1cor7:17

"Let every man abide in the same calling wherein he was called."
1cor7:20

"Brethren, let every man, wherein he is called, therein abide with God."
1cor7:24.

God is willing to restore our lives but you have a part to play in this relationship.

HAVE YOU DISCOVERED GOD's VISION FOR YOUR LIFE?

"A man's gift maketh room for him, and bringeth him before great men."
Proverb 18:16

You have a bigger role to play in fulfilling divine plan. David worked his way into the palace. Joseph's gift took him into the palace. Daniel preserved four seating president because of God's divine plan for his life.

Your gift will make a way for you in the name of Jesus. I will recommend you embrace your calling with joy and solicitude. There is no mountain anywhere, it is only your ignorance that looks like a mountain.

FAVOR CONFESSION

Father thank you for making me righteous and accepted through the blood of Jesus Christ. Because of that, I am blessed and highly favored by God. I am the subject of your affection. Your favor surrounds me as a shield, and the first thing that people see around me is your favored shield.

Thank you that I have favor with you and man today. All day long people go out of their way to bless me and help me. I have favor with everyone that I deal with today. Doors that were once closed are now opened for me.

I receive preferential treatment, and I have special privileges, I am Gods favored child.

No good thing will he withhold from me. Because of Gods favor my enemies cannot triumph over my life. I have supernatural increase and promotion.

I declare restoration to everything that the devil has stolen from my life. I have honor in the midst of my adversaries and an

Chapter 2 - How do I Fulfil God's Vision for my Life?

increase in assets, especially in real estate and expansion of territories.

Because I am highly favored by God, I experience great victories, supernatural turnarounds, and miraculous breakthrough in the midst of great impossibilities. I receive recognition, prominence, and honor.

Petitions are granted to me even by ungodly authorities. Policies, rules, regulations, and laws are changed and reverse on my behalf.

I win battles that I don't even have to fight, because God fights them for me. This is the day, the set time and the designated moment for me to experience the free favor of God, that profusely and lavishly abound on my behalf in Jesus name.

Amen.

YOU MUST BE BORN AGAIN

If you are a born again Christian; we like to encourage you in your Christian life. If you are not a born again Christian we can help you here receive genuine salvation.

"Therefore if any man be in Christ, he is a new creature: old things are passed away; behold, all things are become new." **2cor5:17**

Now repeat this Prayer after me

Say Lord Jesus, I accept you today, as my Lord and my savior, forgive me of my sins wash me with your blood. Right now, I believe, I am sanctified, I am save, I am free, I am free from the Power of sin to serve the Lord Jesus. Thank you Lord for saving me.

Amen.

Congratulations: You are now a born again christian!

Chapter 2 - How do I Fulfil God's Vision for my Life?

What must I do to determine my divine visitation?

To determine divine visitation you must be born again!

The word says as many as received him, to them gave He power to become the sons of God. Even to them that believe on his name.

To qualify for divine visitation do the following sincerely

1) Acknowledge that you are a sinner and that He died for you. **Rom3:23.**

2) Repent of your sins. **Acts 3:19, Luke13:5, 2Peter3:9**

3) Believe in your heart that Jesus died for your sin. **Romans10:10**

4) Confess Jesus as the Lord over your life. **Romans10:10, Acts2:21**

Now repeat this Prayer after me

Say Lord Jesus, I accept you today, as my Lord and my savior, forgive me of my sins wash me with your blood.

Right now, I believe, I am sanctified, I am save, I am free, I am free from the Power of sin to serve the Lord Jesus. Thank you Lord for saving me.

Watch the Spirit of God bear witness with your Spirit confirming His word with signs following. The word says The Spirit itself beareth witness with our spirit, that we are the children of God.

Join a bible believing church or join us on our weekly and Sunday worship services at 343 Sanford Avenue Newark New Jersey 07106.

Chapter 2 - How do I Fulfil God's Vision for my Life?

WISDOM KEYS

- Every Productive Society is a society heading to the top

- Millions of Nigerians run away from Nigeria, very few Nigerians stay in Nigeria.

- My decision to return Nigeria is the will of God for my life

- My short coming in America after 18 years, trained me to be wise, to think, reflect and reason appropriately.

- If you train your mind to reason it will train your hands to earn money.

- It is absurd to use the money of the heathen to build the kingdom of the living God.

- Every Ministry reveals its agenda and goal either at the beginning or at the end. Be careful of your life it is your first Ministry.

- The average American mind is conditioned for a continual quest to get new things and (discard the former) and throw away old things.

- When I considered well, my BMW jeep became my initial deposit for the work of the ministry in Nigeria

- Money will never fall from any Treebank, Treasury Department or person. Make up your mind to be independent today.

- Everyone is waiting for you to change your mind until you change your thinking nothing changes around you.

- Multiple academic degrees in other discipline gave me the chance to think, reflect and reason

- What so everyone are thinking and reflecting at the moment reveals you to the time and the now factor

- All events and intents are the product of precise thought processes, accurate reason every event is designed for a designated timeline

- Wisdom is your ability to think, to create and invent. If you can think wise enough you will come out of penury

Chapter 2 - How do I Fulfil God's Vision for my Life?

- The distance between you and success is your creative ability to think reason and reflect accurate.

- Success is the result of hard work, commitment resolve and determination learning from past mistakes and failing.

- If you organize your mind you have organized your life and destiny.

- There is a thin line between success and failure. If you look above and beyond you are on your way to success.

- Wealth is your ability to think, power is your ability to reason and success is your ability to be informed.

- If you can make use of your mind by thinking and reasoning God will make use of your life and destiny.

- Think and Be Great

- Reflect, Reason, think and be great

- Famous people are born of woman

- That you will make it is your intention; that you will survive is your resolve, that you will succeed with changes is your determination, personal efforts and hard work.

- No man was born a failure. Lack of vision is the end product of failure.

- Working with mental patients encourages and aspire me to be a productive observant and dedicated to my assignment.

- Successful people are not magicians, it is the will power combined with hard work, and determination and a resolve to succeed that make them succeed.

- In the unequivocal state of the mind, intention is not a location or a position it is the state of the mind.

- So many people think that they think. The mind is used to think reflect and reason. You will remain blind with your eye open until you can see with your mind by thinking.

- There is no favoritism in accurate and precise calculation

Chapter 2 - How do I Fulfil God's Vision for my Life?

- Although knowledge is power, information is the key and gateway to a great future.

- It will take the hand of God to move the hand of man.

- With the backing of the great wise God, nothing will disconnect you from your inheritance.

- As long as you have wisdom and understanding of God, Satan and evil cannot manipulate your life and destiny.

- You have come this far by yourself judgment and decision you have made in the past, now lean and listen to God for another dimension of greatness.

- Great people are common people it is extra ordinary effort and the price of sacrifice that produces greatness.

- As a mental direct care worker I saw a great pastor and a motivational speaker within myself.

- Menial job does not reduce your self-worth, until you resolve to achieve greatness see greatness in all you do; you will never count in your community.

- The principle of Jesus will solve your gambling and addiction problems

- The man of Jesus will lead you into heaven,

- Everyone have their self-appraisal and what they think about you. Until you discover yourself other opinion about you will alter the real you.

- Supervisors and directors are just a position in the chain of command in a work place. Never allow your supervisor hierarchy to alter your opinion about yourself.

- Everyone can come out of debt if they make up their mind.

- That I am not a decision maker at work does not diminish my contribution to my world.

Chapter 2 - How do I Fulfil God's Vision for my Life?

- Although it appears like it was a poor decision to accept a direct care employment at a psychiatric hospital as I reflect of my nine years of experience, it became apparent that I have learnt and experienced enough for my next assignment.

- Self-encouragement and determination is a resolve of the heart.

- If you are determined to make a difference, and do the things that make a difference you will eventually make a difference.

- Good things do not come easy

- Short cuts will cut your life short.

- Those who look ahead move ahead.

- Life is all about making an impact. In your life time strive to make an impact in your community.

- Make friends and connect with people who are moving ahead of you in life.

- If you can look around well you have come a long way in your life, made a lot of difference and realized a lot of success in life.

- If you are my old friend, hurry up to reach out to me before I become a stranger to you.

- Everything I am blessed with inspirations from God, that change my definition and interpretation of the world around me.

- I thought I was stagnant and lonely until I looked around and noticed my children running around and my wife cooking.

- At 40 I resigned my Job to seek the Lord forever.

- My ministry took a drastic rise to the top when the wisdom of God visited me with knowledge and understanding.

- You will be a better person if you understand the characteristics of your personality – your mood swings attitudes and habits.

- It is the seed of love you sow into the heart of a child and a woman that you reap in due time.

- Love is not selfish, love share everything including the concealed secrets of the mind.

- As long as you have a prayer life and a bible; you will never feel lonely, rejected and idle in the race of life.

- When good friends disconnect from you, let them go, they might have seen something new in a different direction.

Chapter 2 - How do I Fulfil God's Vision for my Life?

- Confidence in yourself and in God is the only way to bring you out of captivity

- Never train a child to waste his/her time.

- The mind is the greatest assets of a great future.

- You walk by common sense run by principles and fly by instruction.

- Those who fly in flight of life fly alone.

- Up in the air you are alone. No one can toll you accept the compass of knowledge and information

- I have seen a tolling vehicle I have seen a tolling ship I have never seen a tolling airplane.

- I exercise my judgment and make a decision every minute of the day.

- Decisions are crucial, critical and vital with reference to your future.

- So many people wish for a great future. You can only work towards a great future.

- Your celebrity status began when you discovered your talent. What are you good at? Work at it with all commitment.

- Prayers will sustain you but the wisdom of God will prosper you.

- When I met Oyedepo, his teachings changed my perspective, but when I met Ibiyeomie; His teaching changed my perception.

- I will be successful in ministry if only I concentrate and focus my energy in the work of the ministry.

- It took the late Dr. Vincent Pearle Norman's book to open my mind towards kingdom success.

CHAPTER 3

PRAYER OF SALVATION

It will profit us nothing as a ministry if after reading this book, your salvation is still questionable. I long to see you saved and delivered from all the wiles and schemes of the devil.

ARE YOU SAVED?

The honest truth is that the Lord Jesus really does not know you unless you are saved. For as many as are led by the Spirit of God, they are the sons of God. For ye have not received the spirit of bondage again to fear; but ye have received the Spirit of adoption, whereby we cry, Abba, Father. The Spirit itself beareth witness with our spirit, that we are the children of God. **Romans 8:14-16**

What must I do to determine my divine visitation?

To determine divine visitation you must be born again. The word says as many as received him, to them gave he power to become the sons of God. Even to them that believe on his name.

To qualify for divine visitation do the following sincerely,

1) Acknowledge that you are a sinner and that He died for you. **Rom3:23.**

2) Repent of your sins. **Acts 3:19, Luke13:5, 2Peter3:9**

3) Believe in your heart that Jesus died for your sin. **Romans10:10**

4) Confess Jesus as the Lord over your life. **Romans10:10, Acts2:21.**

Chapter 3 - Prayer of Salvation

Now repeat this Prayer after me

Say Lord Jesus, I accept you today, as my Lord and my savior, forgive me of my sins wash me with your blood. Right now, I believe, I am sanctified, I am save, I am free, I am free from the Power of sin to serve the Lord Jesus. Thank you Lord for saving me. **Amen.**

Congratulations

YOU ARE NOW A BORN AGAIN CHRISTIAN

AGAIN I SAY TO YOU CONGRATULATIONS

I adjure you to watch the Spirit of God bear witness with your Spirit confirming His word with signs following. The word says The Spirit itself beareth witness with our spirit, that we are the children of God.

MIRACLE CARE OUTREACH

"…But that the members should have the same care one for another"
1cor12:25

We are all members of the body of Christ. Jesus commanded us to love our neighbor as ourselves. This includes caring for one another as a member of one body. True love is expressed in caring and giving. The word says for God so Love He gave….

Reach out to someone in need of Jesus, help someone in crisis find Christ. Look out and prove your love to Jesus by caring and inviting your friends and associates to find Jesus the Healer.

Invite your friends to our Home Care Cell Fellowship (Miracle chapel Intl Satellite fellowship) In the USA at 33 Schley Street Newark New Jersey 07112.

If you are in Nigeria—**MIRACLE OF GOD MINISTRIES**

A.K.A"MIRACLE CHAPEL INTL"
Mpama –Egbu-Owerri Imo state Nigeria.

Chapter 3 - Prayer of Salvation

(Home Care Cell fellowship Group). We meet every Tuesday at 6:00pm-7:00pm.

LIFE IS NOT ALL ABOUT DURATION BUT ITS ALL ABOUT DONATION

What does the above statement mean?....

"Life consists not in accumulation of material wealth"
Luke12:15.

"But it's all about liberality....meaning-what you can give and share with others."
Proverb11:25.

When you live for others--You live forever-because you out live your generation by the legacy you live behind after you depart into glory to be with the Lord.

But when you live to yourself - you are reduced to self—you are easily forgotten when you die and depart in glory. Permit me to admonish you today to live your life to be a blessing to a soul connected to you today.

I want you to know that so many souls are connected and looking up to you, and through you so many souls will be saved and rescued from destruction.

Will you disciple someone today to find Jesus Christ?

As a genuine Christian; it is your duty to evangelize Jesus Christ to all you meet on your way. Jesus is still in the healing business-Jesus is still doing miracles from time of old to now. Therefore tell someone about Jesus Christ today, disciple and bring them to Church.

John 1:45 Philip findeth Nathanael....

Please to prove the sincerity of your love for God today; please become a soul winner. The dignity of your Christianity is hidden in your boldness to proclaim and evangelize Jesus Christ to all you meet on your way.

There is a question mark on the integrity of your Christianity until you become a life soul winner. Invite someone to join us worship the Lord Jesus this coming Sunday. **Amen**

Chapter 3 - Prayer of Salvation

MIRACLE OF GOD MINISTRIES

PILLARS OF THE COMMISSION

We Believe Preach and Practice the following,

1) We believe and preach Salvation to every living human being

2) We believe and preach Repentance and forgiveness of sins

3) We believe and preach the baptism of the Holy Spirit and Spiritual gifts

4) We believe and teach the Prosperity

5) We believe and preach Divine Healing and Miracles (Signs &Wonder)

6) We believe and preach Faith

7) We believe and Proclaim the Power of God (Supernatural)

8) We believe and Proclaim Praise & Worship to God

9) We believe and preach Wisdom

10) We believe and preach Holiness (Consecration)

11) We believe and preach Vision

12) We believe and teach the Word of God

13) We believe and teach Success

14) We believe and practice Prayer

15) We believe and teach Deliverance

This 15 stones form the Pillars of Our Commission.

Become part of this church family and follow this great move of God.

Chapter 3 - Prayer of Salvation

MY HEART FELT PRAYER FOR YOU

I long to see meet God through one of our channels, either through this book, or through our DVD, or sermons taped and recorded.

Now let me Pray for you:

O Lord God that heareth prayer, unto thee shall all flesh come. Lord Jesus, restore this precious soul that is reading this destiny restoration pillars. May their lives, career, and destiny accelerate like never before.

May you grant them their heart desires and make all their plans to succeed. Give them a testimony that will forever give them reason to praise and glorify your Holy Name.

Amen.

****DO NOT FORGET YOUR GOD****

" Then beware lest thou forget the Lord, which brought thee forth out of the land of Egypt, from the house of bondage."
Deut 6:12

In my own opinion knowing God is a personal thing.

We are instructed to *"....work out your own salvation with fear and trembling. For it is God which worketh in you both to will and to do of his good pleasure."*
Phil 2:12-13

It is my vision to see you experience a personal encounter with our Lord Jesus Christ. A lot of church folks have indirectly denied him, but I tell you the truth as long as you embrace him invisibly, he will do great things in your life. We must always practice the ritual of daily devotion and prayer as a lifestyle.

Chapter 3 - Prayer of Salvation

You can join our prayer-line 515-739-1216-code 162288 every Mondays, Wednesday, and Saturdays eastern time.

More also you can come worship with us together at our worship center 343 Sanford avenue Newark New Jersey 07106.

Always remember God is spirit, therefore we must worship him in spirit and in truth. God is not a man that he should lie, nor the son of man that he should repent.

~ Learn to honor the presence of God in your life.. ~

Embrace the acts and hand of God in your life.

~Respect and reverence God in your life time. ~

Help spread the gospel of Jesus by winning soul for the Kingdom of God.

Finally I must talk to you about eternity! Heaven is real and we all must make conscious plan to make it at last. I hate to tell you more about hell but we must repent of our sins forsake our sins confess Jesus as Lord and embrace the gift of Salvation for us to make heaven. We must live a righteous life, worthy of emulation for others to copy for the Kingdom of God.

ETERNITY IS REAL

It will profit us nothing as a ministry if you finish reading this book without making plans for heaven. You must make conscious plans to make heaven because eternity is real.

Indeed we live in an immoral time, sin has gained grounds and promotion that even the righteous are tempted to fall short of the glory of God.

Indeed we live in an immoral time, sin has gained grounds and promotion that even

Chapter 3 - Prayer of Salvation

the righteous are tempted to fall short of the glory of God.

You might ask me, what must I do to be saved?

As long as we believe and repent God is willing to forgive and to restore our lives *"And they said, Believe on the Lord Jesus Christ, and thou shalt be saved, and thy house."*
Acts16:31.

"Salvation is possible only through the name of our Lord Jesus Christ. Neither is there salvation in any other: for there is none other name under heaven given among men, whereby we must be saved."
Acts4:12.

I admonish you therefore to think twice before you commit those sins that not only easily beset you but also separates you far away from God. As long as you repent even now, God is more than willing to restore and save your life from eternal hell fire.

And make straight paths for your feet, lest that which is lame be turned out of the way; but let it rather be healed. Follow peace with all men, and holiness, without which no man shall see the Lord.

Hebrew 12:13-14.

Make conscious plans to make heaven. Change the way you approach things and God will restore and forgive you of all your sins. **Amen**

CHAPTER 4
ABOUT THE AUTHOR

Rev Franklin N Abazie is the founding and Presiding Pastor of Miracle of God Ministries with headquarters in Newark, New Jersey USA and a branch church in Owerri- Imo State Nigeria. He is following the footsteps of one of his mentors, Oral Roberts (Healing Evangelist) of the blessed memory.

The Lord passed Oral Roberts healing mantle two days before he went to be with the Lord at age 91 into the hand of healing evangelist-Rev Franklin N Abazie in a vision.

In all his services the Power and Presence of God is present to heal all in his audience. He is an ordained man of God with a Healing Ministry reviving the healing and miracle ministry of Jesus Christ of Nazareth.

Pastor Franklin N Abazie, is called by God with a unique mandate:

"THE MOMENT IS DUE TO IMPACT YOUR WORLD THROUGH THE REVIVAL OF THE HEALING & MIRACLE MINISTRY OF JESUS CHRIST OF NAZARETH
I AM SENDING YOU TO RESTORE HEALTH UNTO THEE AND I WILL HEAL THEE OF THY WOUNDS. SAID THE LORD OF HOST"

He is a gifted ardent Teacher of the word of God who operates also in the office of a Prophet, generating and attracting undeniable signs & wonders, special miracles and healings, with apostolic fireworks of the Holy Ghost.

He is the founding and presiding senior Pastor of this fast growing Healing ministry.

Chapter 4 - About the Author

He has written over 86 inspirational, healing and transforming books covering almost all aspect of divine healing and life. He is happily married and blessed with children.

BOOKS BY REV FRANKLIN N ABAZIE

1) Commanding Abundance
2) The outcome of faith
3) Understanding the secret of prevailing prayers
4) Understanding the secret of the man God uses
5) Activating my due Season
6) Overcoming Divine Verdicts
7) The Outcome of Divine Wisdom
8) Understanding God's Restoration Mandate
9) Walking in the Victory and Authority of the truth
10) Gods Covenant Exemption
11) Destiny Restoration Pillars
12) Provoking Acceptable Praise
13) Understanding Divine Judgment
14) Activating Angelic Re-enforcement
15) Provoking Un-Merited Favor
16) The Benefits of the Speaking faith
17) Understanding Divine Arrangement

18) Understanding Divine Healing
19) The Mystery of Endurance
20) Obeying Divine Instructions
21) Understanding the Voice of God
22) Never give up on Hope
23) The prevailing Power of faith
24) Understanding Divine Prosperity
25) The Reward of Prayer
26) Covenant Keys to Answered Prayers
27) Activating the Forces of Vengeance
28) Put your faith to work
29) Where is your trust?
30) The Audacity of the Blood of Jesus
31) Redeeming Your Days
32) The force of Vision
33) Breaking the shackles of Family Curses
34) Wisdom for Marriage Stability
35) The winners Faith
36) The Prayer solution
37) The power of Prayer
38) Prayer strategy
39) The prayer that works
40) Walking in Forgiveness
41) The power of the grace of God

42) The power of Persistence
43) Overcoming Divine verdicts
44) The audacity of the blood of Jesus.
45) The prevailing power of the blood of Jesus
46) The benefit of the speaking faith.
47) Fearless faith
48) Redeeming Your Days.
49) The Supernatural Power of Prophecy
50) The companionship of the Holy Spirit
51) Understanding Divine Judgement
52) Understanding Divine Prosperity
53) Dominating Controlling Forces
54) The winners Faith
55) Destiny Restoration Pillars
56) Developing Spiritual Muscles
57) Inexplicable faith
58) The lifestyle of Prayer
59) Developing a positive attitude in life.
60) The mystery of Divine supply
61) Encounter with God's Power
62) Walking in love
63) Praying in the Spirit
64) How to provoke your testimony

65) Walking in the reality of the Anointing
66) The reality of new birth
67) The price of freedom
68) The Supernatural power of faith
69) The Power of Persistence
70) The intellectual components of Redemption
71) Overcoming Fear
72) The Force of Vision
73) Overcoming Prevailing Challenges
74) The Power of the Grace of God
75) My life & Ministry
76) The Mystery of Praise

MIRACLE OF GOD MINISTRIES

NIGERIA CRUSADE 2012

MIRACLE OF GOD MINISTRIES
NIGERIA CRUSADE 2012

MIRACLE OF GOD MINISTRIES

NIGERIA CRUSADE

2012

MIRACLE OF GOD MINISTRIES

NIGERIA CRUSADE

2012

www.ingramcontent.com/pod-product-compliance
Lightning Source LLC
Chambersburg PA
CBHW021445080526
44588CB00009B/690